FRONT SEAT EDITION

P9-DZA-276

CHRISTMAS Sing·Along CAR·I·OKE

WORKMAN PUBLISHING
www.workman.com

Songs for the Whole Family • Includes the Words to All 19 Recorded Songs and Choreography for the Nutcracker Backseat Ballet, plus Bonus Lyrics and Christmas Trivia Throughout

CHRISTMAS
Sing·Along
CAR·I·OKE

David ⊕ Schiller

Illustrated by Tim Robinson

WORKMAN PUBLISHING · NEW YORK

To Romie, for showing us the joy of belting it out.
And, as always, for Asa, Quinn, Theo, and Clara.

Copyright © 2005 by David Schiller

Illustrations © 2005 by Tim Robinson

Published simultaneously in Canada
by Thomas Allen & Son Limited.

Library of Congress Cataloging-in-Publication Data is available.

ISBN-13: 978-0-7611-3984-3
ISBN-10: 0-7611-3984-2

Workman books are available at special discounts when
purchased in bulk for premiums and sales promotions
as well as for fund-raising or educational use.
Special editions or book excerpts can also be created to specification.
For details, contact the Special Sales Director at the address below.

Workman Publishing Company
708 Broadway
New York, NY 10003-9555
www.workman.com

Printed in China

First printing: October 2005

10 9 8 7 6 5 4 3 2 1

CONTENTS

CATCH THE SPIRIT!

THE STUFF OF FAMILY MEMORIES

Nothing moves the holiday spirit like Christmas music. We become aware of these songs when very young, remember them all our lives, and respond to them as welcome friends. Overhear a few bars of "Silent Night" or even the jingling sleigh bells of "Jingle Bells," and a cold, gray December day is transformed. Attend the school holiday sing, take the family to a performance of Handel's *Messiah,* or watch carolers at the mall, and suddenly the world lights up, full of joy and promise.

Singing Christmas songs is best of all, radiating all that good feeling. CHRISTMAS SING-ALONG CAR-I-OKE brings the whole family together in song and activity for a good old-fashioned family sing-along. It's got the music, it's got the words, and it's got directions, tips, stories, and fun things to do to make car trips even livelier.

Like its predecessor, *All-American Car-i-oke,* CHRISTMAS SING-ALONG CAR-I-OKE is inspired by two musical ideas: the fun of singing

IT WASN'T ALWAYS THIS WAY

Christmas and music have always been entwined—as far back as A.D.129, long before Christmas was officially Christmas! But the fact is that until fairly recently, Christmas caroling wasn't considered respectable in certain corners of society. The people loved singing. Church leaders hated it because they thought the songs weren't religious enough. Then, in 1223, St. Francis of Assisi invited common folk to sing Christmas songs during the first living nativity displays, spurring a wave of popular Christmas carols or "canticles." But rigid officials were

shocked by the tunes' coarse folk origins and Biblically incorrect verses. Another problem arose because caroling evolved into a sectarian pastime known as minstrelsy. Come December, rowdy groups traveled through the countryside singing drinking songs and other less than holy music, causing church leaders to fear that the spirit of Christmas was being wrested away from the devout. Only gradually did the two sides come together. By the mid-nineteenth century, the respectable groups of carolers that we think of today became popular, and church leaders finally welcomed the role of music in bringing the holiday to life.

together, and the phenomenon of karaoke, which began in Japan in the 1970s and soon reached America.

It's also, in a way, a reaction to what's happening more and more on family trips: The kids are in the backseat, watching a DVD or plugged into a game player, and the parents sit up front, watching the miles go by and maybe arguing about when to stop. But here's a crazy thought: Why not enjoy travel time as family time? After all, how often is it that you are all really together? Car-i-oke is a great way to interact, laugh, maybe do a front seat vs. backseat talent show contest, see who can hit the high notes—*and* get into the holiday spirit. Exactly the kind of stuff that family memories are made of.

Hopefully, you'll find many of your favorite Christmas carols in the pages ahead. We've chosen some especially for little kids— "Must Be Santa" and "Jingle Bells." For big kids—"The Twelve Days of Christmas," with its fill-in-the-blank word play, and a hip-hop version of "'Twas the Night Before Christmas." There are some to challenge the real singers in your car—"Silent Night," the "Hallelujah" chorus. And lots of traditional songs to transport you to a snowy night, gathered outside with friends and family, singing from house to house.

The key to Car-i-oke is to take it slow. Older kids in those eye-rolling teenage years might not even join in for a song or two. And don't be afraid to hit the replay button on your CD player. Singing to recorded music is not exactly natural for most of us.

Oh, and one final note. Even though it's *Car*-i-oke, it works just as well wherever you have a CD player and a group of willing singers. So when your whole family gathers for Christmas, here's an instant caroling party. Happy Holidays!

A SINGER'S TOOLBOX

Hitting the right notes may be the most obvious skill of a professional singer, and our inability to sing on pitch consistently may be the biggest frustration to the rest of us. But to paraphrase Oscar Wilde, "Anyone can sing in tune. *I* sing with wonderful expression." Here are a few tips for more effective singing.

POSTURE

Although it's a given that you're sitting and not standing (which is the best position for singing), a few things to pay attention to include:

1. Sit up straight, with your spine nicely extended.
2. Keep your head centered over your shoulders and your chin level.
3. Relax your shoulders and arms.

BREATHING

1. Breathe deeply, low into the body.
2. Keep your throat open and chin relaxed. (To know what an open throat feels like, concentrate on the feeling you have the next time you yawn—but just before you open your mouth.)
3. Whenever possible, take a breath at least a beat before you start to sing.

4. Inhale with your ribs open and up; exhale from your diaphragm.

THE SONG

1. Think of the words as a story: Who is telling the story? Where does it take place? What is the story about?
2. Note the natural pauses; this is where you'll be able to catch a new breath.
3. If you're unfamiliar with the song, listen to the music, tap out the rhythm with your foot, and hum along using nonsense syllables.

One last tip that all the kids will love: Just before you start to sing, open up your voice by pretending you're Mr. Ed and blowing through loose lips until they start flapping and making a horse sound. Now you're ready!

ALL TOGETHER NOW

WE WISH YOU A MERRY CHRISTMAS

TRACK **1**

This cheerful English song with its playful, upbeat lyrics has been a favorite of carolers since caroling began. And that's about all we know about the song's history. The word music historians use for songs like this is "traditional," meaning that the authorship is unknown and that the song has been passed down from generation to generation pretty much intact. Back in the seventeenth century, which is when this song probably originated, Christmas was a much more raucous affair, and the bands of revelers that went from great house to great house singing had definite expectations of being treated to food and drink. Hence the lyrics "Now bring us some figgy pudding" and "We won't go until we get some." They meant it!

Which is a fun way to approach singing "We Wish You a Merry Christmas." Put an insistent tone into those verses, and become more demanding with each repeat.

SO WHAT IS THIS "FIGGY PUDDING"?

We demand it when singing "We Wish You a Merry Christmas." We read about it in Dickens's *A Christmas Carol,* as Mary Cratchit serves one to her family. But don't expect a soft, custardy treat. An English pudding is a dense and cakelike dessert. It's often quite dramatic, too. Traditional plum pudding is made a year in advance in a high, dome-

shaped mold, then is doused in brandy and brought flaming to the table. Baked into the pudding are silver coins (for luck) and symbolic trinkets (find a ring in your serving and you'll be married within the year; find a thimble and you'll stay single). Figgy pudding is made with dried Calimyrna or other figs, plus spices such as cinnamon and nutmeg.

Over the years, "We Wish You a Merry Christmas" has evolved into a sign-off, a way of saying have a great holiday, as the group of carolers moves on to its next stop. But we're making it our first song. It's one of the easiest ones to sing, and it's a perfect way to get into the holiday singing mood.

WE WISH YOU A MERRY CHRISTMAS

First verse:
We wish you a merry Christmas,
We wish you a merry Christmas,
We wish you a merry Christmas,
And a happy New Year!

Repeat first verse

Bridge:
Glad tidings we bring
To you and your kin;
Glad tidings for Christmas
And a happy New Year!

Second verse:
Now bring us some figgy pudding,
Now bring us some figgy pudding,
 Now bring us some figgy pudding,
 And a cup of good cheer!

2

Third verse:

We won't go until we get some,
We won't go until we get some,
We won't go until we get some,
So bring it out here!

Repeat first verse

JOY TO THE KIDS!

Christmas gotten too commercial? Only a toymaker would dispute it. Still, anyone who has kids, or remembers being a kid, knows that for children, the best part of Christmas lies in a pile under the tree. But guess what? For nearly two thousand years, holiday gifts—if they were given at all— came on New Year's, or sometimes January 6th (the 12th day of Christmas). Things only started changing, in America, after the publication of Clement Moore's "'Twas the Night Before Christmas" (see page 22) and Charles

JOY TO THE WORLD

TRACK **2**

There's no such thing as a Tin Pan Alley of religious music, but the story of "Joy to the World" does make you wonder—between them, the lyricist and composer were responsible for 2,100 hymns! But unlike those twentieth-century songwriting teams based in New York's famous Brill Building, this team didn't even live in the same century, let alone on the same continent. Celebrated English hymnist Isaac Watts wrote the words in 1719. The American composer Lowell Mason—called the Father of American Church and Public School Music—published an arrangement of the music in 1839. And in another preview of contemporary music, Mason "sampled" the work of another composer in arranging "Joy"—that of George Frideric Handel, whom you may know from a popular Christmas number called the *Messiah!*

Feel like shaking things up a bit? "Joy to the World" is a great front-seat/backseat song. The front seat can take the first three lines of each verse, with their stately, booming melody full of pronouncements. Then the backseat can take the second three verses, which are even more fun to sing—first they murmur along for two repeating lines, then suddenly shoot up and glide back to earth.

4

JOY TO THE WORLD

First verse:

Joy to the world, the Lord is come!
Let earth receive her King;
Let ev'ry heart prepare Him room,
And heav'n and nature sing,
And heav'n and nature sing,
And heav'n, and heav'n and nature sing.

Second verse:

Joy to the world, the Savior reigns!
Let men their songs employ;
While fields and floods, rocks, hills and plains
Repeat the sounding joy,
Repeat the sounding joy,
Repeat, repeat the sounding joy.

Third verse:

He rules the world with truth and grace,
And makes the nations prove
The glories of His righteousness,
And wonders of His love,
And wonders of His love,
And wonders, wonders of His love.

Dickens's *A Christmas Carol,* which gave kids the idea to *expect* presents from Santa on Christmas or Christmas Eve. Soon shrewd merchants obliged, and in the years after the Civil War, retailers brought Santas into their stores, offered holiday specials, and created a Christmas shopping season that lasted two weeks. By World War II, when presents needed to arrive overseas in time for Christmas for American soldiers, the season was expanded to four weeks, with the traditional kick-off— as it is today—on "Black Friday," the day after Thanksgiving.

AT HOME, IN A MANGER

A nativity scene, also called a manger scene or a crèche, is a very familiar sight at the holidays, and one of the few decorative touches that hearkens back to the Bible. Interestingly, it is also directly the work of one of the most beloved Christian figures, St. Francis of Assisi. Envisioning his display as a living teaching tool, St. Francis constructed a manger scene in 1223 outside of his church in Italy, using real people to play the various roles and inviting the children to view it from the inside out while he chanted the Gospel. From this original work come both the living nativities—complete with

ANGELS WE HAVE HEARD ON HIGH

TRACK 3

Like "O Holy Night," this carol originated in France as an eighteenth-century hymn ("Les anges dans nos compagnes"). Legend has it that the tune was one used by shepherds in southern France, who had a custom of calling to one another on Christmas Eve, using the refrain "Gloria in Excelsis Deo." Finally published in English in 1875, it became a favorite carol, probably because of the vocal acrobatics involved in singing the "Gloria" refrain.

ANGELS WE HAVE HEARD ON HIGH

First verse:
Angels we have heard on high,
Sweetly singing o'er the plains;
And the mountains in reply,
Echoing their joyous strains.

Chorus:
Glo — ria,
In Excelsis Deo!
Glo — ria,
In Excelsis Deo!

Second verse:
Shepherd, why this jubilee?
Why your joyous strains prolong?
What the gladsome tidings be,
Which inspire your heavenly song?

Repeat chorus

Third verse:
Come to Bethlehem and see,
Him whose birth the angels sing.
Come adore on bended knee,
Christ the Lord, the newborn King.

Repeat chorus

Fourth verse:
See Him in a manger laid,
Whom the choirs of angels praise.
Mary, Joseph, lend your aid,
While our hearts in love we raise.

Repeat chorus

live animals, straw, even newborn infants—that are the centerpieces of many church celebrations, and the lawn crèches and smaller, carved crib scenes that people create at home.

THE HOLLY, AND THE IVY, TOO

Decking the halls with greenery is an ancient pagan custom that evolved into a Christmas tradition. As far back as Roman times, evergreens such as holly and ivy symbolized good luck and were given as gifts during Saturnalia, the winter solstice festival. Later the Church found it easy to make holly a Christian symbol, using its needle-sharp leaves and blood-red berries to represent

DECK THE HALLS

TRACK 4

Every year comes the challenge—to get in the Christmas spirit early enough to enjoy the holiday. If you listen to most people, though, finding the spirit of the season is getting harder. Maybe there's an antidote right under our noses: "Deck the Halls," a merry revelry lit by the blazing Yule log and filled with a well-dressed chorus of voices. It's got an easy, catchy melody (Mozart once appropriated it for a violin and piano duet), and with its fa-la-las and rhyming iambs—holly and jolly, apparel and carol—it's one of those songs that's enormously satisfying to sing. "Deck the Halls" was first published in London in 1784 with Welsh lyrics under the title "Nos Galan," which means "New Year's Night." In fact, the third verse is about hailing the New Year. The English words we sing today were written later, in the nineteenth century, around the time of Dickens's *A Christmas Carol.*

DECK THE HALLS

First verse:

Deck the halls with boughs of holly,
Fa la la la la, la la la la.
'Tis the season to be jolly,
Fa la la la la, la la la la.
Don we now our gay apparel,
Fa la la, la la la, la la la.

8

Troll the ancient Yuletide carol,
Fa la la la la, la la la la.

Second verse:
See the blazing Yule before us,
Fa la la la la, la la la la.
Strike the harp and join the chorus.
Fa la la la la, la la la la.
Follow me in merry measure,
Fa la la, la la la, la la la.
While I tell of Yuletide treasure,
Fa la la la la, la la la la.

Third verse:
Fast away the old year passes,
Fa la la la la, la la la la.
Hail the new, ye lads and lasses,
Fa la la la la, la la la la.
Sing we joyous, all together,
Fa la la, la la la, la la la.
Heedless of the wind and
    weather,
Fa la la la la, la la la la.

Christ's crown of
thorns. But ivy, with
its strong association
with Bacchus, Roman
god of wine, still
speaks to the pagan
side of the holiday
celebration.

MUST BE SANTA

TRACK **5**

Any *really* little kids in the car? "Must Be Santa" is the perfect first carol, with no reading required. In fact, it's based on a traditional German question-and-answer song sung between teachers and students, with singers exercising their memories by recalling an ever-growing string of lines. The children's music superstar Raffi implicitly understood the song's spell of interactive fun when he added it to his all-time bestselling album, *Singable Songs for the Very Young* (1976), and introduced the Christmas classic to yet another generation of kids (and parents).

MUST BE SANTA

First verse:

Who's got a beard that's long and white?
Santa's got a beard that's long and white!
Who comes around on a special night?
Santa comes around on a special night!
Special night, beard that's white—
Must be Santa,
Must be Santa,
Must be Santa, Santa Claus!

Second verse:

Who wears boots and a suit of red?
Santa wears boots and a suit of red!
Who wears a long cap on his head?
Santa wears a long cap on his head!
Cap on head, suit that's red—
Special night, beard that's white—
Must be Santa,
Must be Santa,
Must be Santa, Santa Claus!

MUST BE MUSIC

Paul McCartney famously cannot read music. Irving Berlin, who towers above even The Beatles for writing great popular songs, could compose only in the key of F. And Hal Moore, creator of "Must Be Santa" and dozens of other songs, didn't even play music. As his son, the singer-songwriter Tim Moore says, "He was really musical. He could whistle new melodies over any music. He just never learned to play an instrument, so he collaborated with people who could play and write music."

A pioneer of American radio, Hal Moore hoboed the southern railways as a teenager. Then at age twenty, he tried radio announcing. Within three years he was a CBS staff announcer in New York. As one of America's first DJs on New York's legendary WNEW, he met and worked with most of the great singers of his era. In 1960, Moore wrote "Must Be Santa" with musician Bill Fredericks and played it for Mitch Miller, a producer for Columbia Records who had his own chorus and TV show. Miller loved it and recorded it for his first and only holiday album.

Third verse:

Who's got a big red cherry nose?
Santa's got a big red cherry nose!
Who laughs this way: HO, HO, HO?
Santa laughs this way: HO, HO, HO!
HO HO HO, cherry nose—
Cap on head, suit that's red—
Special night, beard that's white—
Must be Santa,
Must be Santa,
Must be Santa, Santa Claus!

Fourth verse:

Who very soon will come our way?
Santa very soon will come our way!
Eight little reindeer pull his sleigh,
Santa's little reindeer pull his sleigh.
Reindeer sleigh, come our way—
HO, HO, HO, cherry nose—
Cap on head, suit that's red—
Special night, beard that's white—
Must be Santa,
Must be Santa,
Must be Santa, Santa Claus!

BROTHERHOOD OF THE FUR

You see them in the mall. You see them on street corners. You see them at parties. Here are a few facts about America's Santas:

- More than 40,000 men throughout North America don (or dye!) a beard and work as Santas during the holidays.
- Top Santas earn as much as $60,000 in a season.
- Only the fit need apply: Santas often start right after Halloween and routinely work twelve-hour days.
- One booking agency gives its prospective Santas a 260-page manual that outlines everything from how to bleach a beard to what to say when a child asks for his deceased grandmother back.
- Costume tip for Santa wanna-be's: Buy a pair of black steel-toe boots to protect your foot when kids jump off Santa's lap!

GOOD KING WENCESLAS

First published in England in an 1853 collection, *Carols for Christmastide,* "Good King Wenceslas" became such an instant favorite that many people mistook it for an ancient English folksong recently revived. They were partially right; the tune *was* a traditional one, but it was Swedish and had appeared three hundred years earlier as the melody for a "springtime carol." As for the words, they'd been freshly composed by a remarkable clergyman named John Mason Neale, whose many original hymns and translations went far toward promoting the popularity of Christmas carols.

For "Wenceslas," Neale drew upon the legend of the real Duke of Wenceslaus, who ruled Bohemia (now part of Germany) from A.D. 928 to 935. The Duke's kindness was legendary throughout his kingdom, particularly for the charitable deeds he performed on December 26th, St. Stephen's Day. John Mason Neale's unusual poem—it is neither a hymn nor a sacred song—recounts one such incident, and alludes to Wenceslaus's saintliness in the holy heat from his footsteps. Neale considered it nothing less than an act of providence to discover the ancient Swedish tune just as he finished his verses—they each had the same atypical, lilting meter.

GOOD KING WENCESLAS

First verse:

Good King Wenceslas looked out
On the feast of Stephen.
When the snow lay round about
Deep and crisp and even.
Brightly shone the moon that night
Though the frost was cruel;
When a poor man came in sight
Gath'ring winter fuel.

Second verse:

"Hither, page, and stand by me
If thou know'st it, telling:
Yonder peasant, who is he?
Where and what his dwelling?"
"Sire, he lives a good league hence
Underneath the mountain.
Right against the forest fence
By Saint Agnes' fountain."

Third verse:

"Bring me flesh and bring me wine,
Bring me pine logs hither.
Thou and I will see him dine,

ST. STEPHEN'S DAY

So who is this Stephen whose feast day, December 26th, is the setting for "Good King Wenceslas"? None other than the very first martyr of the Christian church. Ordained as a deacon by Jesus' apostles to help look after widows and the poor, Stephen was a wise, angelic figure who worked

miracles and converted many to The Way, as the early church was called. For this, enemies of the church stoned him to death. But Stephen urged God to forgive his killers, only further proving his saintliness and spirit of charity. Throughout the English-speaking world (except the United States), St. Stephen's Day is also Boxing Day, a tradition started centuries ago when the Church opened boxes of alms for the needy on the day after Christmas.

When we bear him thither."
Page and monarch forth they went,
Forth they went together.
Through the rude wind's wild lament
And the bitter weather.

Fourth verse:
"Sire, the night is darker now
And the wind blows stronger.
Fails my heart, I know not how,
I can go no longer."
"Mark my footsteps, my good page,
Tread thou in them boldly.
Thou shalt find the winter's rage
Freeze thy blood less coldly."

Fifth verse:
In his master's steps he trod,
Where the snow lay dinted.
Heat was in the very sod,
Which the Saint had printed.
Therefore, Christian men, be sure
Wealth or rank possessing.
Ye who now will bless the poor
Shall yourselves find blessing.

GO, TELL IT ON THE MOUNTAIN

TRACK **7**

Ready to start clapping your hands? Christmas songs come in a lot of different moods: tender, reverential, nostalgic, merry, whimsical. And then there's the flavor that's best called "rousing." An African-American spiritual, "Go, Tell It on the Mountain" is a powerful trumpet blast of good news.

GO, TELL IT ON THE MOUNTAIN

First verse:
While shepherds kept their watching,
Over silent flocks by night
Behold throughout the heavens,
There shone a holy light.

Refrain:
Go, tell it on the mountain,
Over the hills and everywhere;
Go, tell it on the mountain,
That Jesus Christ is born.

Dating from the early 1800s, "Go, Tell It on the Mountain" was popularized late in that century by the Fisk University Jubilee Singers, a celebrated chorus that still exists, traveling the United States and Europe to raise scholarship funds for Nashville's Fisk University. With this song, unless you're traveling in a bus full of people, you're going to have to sing with enthusiasm to make up for the lack of a large choral sound. But you're Car-i-oke Carolers—you can do it.

Second verse:
The shepherds feared and trembled,
When lo! above the earth
Rang out the angels' chorus
That hailed the Savior's birth.

Repeat refrain

Third verse:
Down in a lowly manger,
The humble Christ was born
And God sent us salvation,
That blessèd Christmas morn.

Repeat refrain

Fourth verse:
When I was a seeker,
I sought both night and day;
I sought the Lord to help me,
And he showed me the way.

Repeat refrain

JINGLE BELLS

TRACK **8**

What would Christmas be without "Jingle Bells"? Yet this top-ten Christmas song never even mentions Christmas. Or the nativity. Or even a whisper about a holiday. Written by James S. Pierpont, a New Englander, "Jingle Bells" started life in 1857 as a song called "The One-Horse Open Sleigh" to be performed on Thanksgiving by Pierpont's father's Sunday school class. It was so popular with the kids that they requested to sing it again at Christmas, and the pairing of holiday and song began. Later, a friend of Mr. Pierpont's called it a "merry little jingle," prompting the name change to "Jingle Bells."

JINGLE BELLS

First verse:

Dashing through the snow
In a one-horse open sleigh,
Over the fields we go,
Laughing all the way;
Bells on bob-tail ring,
Making spirits bright,
What fun it is to ride and sing
A sleighing song tonight!

BEATLES BELLS

Even The Beatles recorded "Jingle Bells," and it's worth searching the attic to find a copy. Each year until they broke up, the Fab Four issued a Christmas record of songs and skits to members of the Official Beatles Fan Club. The records were released as a flexidisc—a kind of flimsy 45. "Jingle Bells" is from 1964's *Another Beatles Christmas Record.*

JINGLE ALL THE WAY

Though popular when it was published, "Jingle Bells" really took off in the twentieth century. Glenn Miller had the country swinging to it in 1941, and in 1943, Bing Crosby and the Andrews Sisters did a version that sold a million copies. A list of other musicians who recorded it reads like a who's who: Barry Manilow, the Beach Boys, Benny Goodman, Bobby Vinton, Booker T. & the MGs, Count Basie, Dean Martin, Duke Ellington, Ella Fitzgerald, Elvis Presley, Frank Sinatra, John Denver, Johnny

Chorus:
Jingle bells, jingle bells,
Jingle all the way!
O what fun it is to ride
In a one-horse open sleigh!

Repeat

Second verse:
A day or two ago,
I thought I'd take a ride,
And soon Miss Fanny Bright
Was seated by my side;
The horse was lean and lank;
Misfortune seemed his lot;
He got into a drifted bank,
And we, we got upsot.

Repeat chorus

Third verse:
A day or two ago,
The story I must tell
I went out on the snow
And on my back I fell;

A gent was riding by
In a one-horse open sleigh,
He laughed as there
I sprawling lie,
But quickly drove away.

Repeat chorus

Fourth verse:
Now the ground is white
Go it while you're young,
Take the girls tonight
And sing this sleighing song;
Just get a bob-tailed bay
Two-forty as his speed
Hitch him to an open sleigh
And crack! you'll take the lead.

Repeat chorus

Cash, Johnny Mathis, Johnny Mercer, Julie Andrews, Les Paul, Nat King Cole, Oscar Peterson, Pat Boone, Patti Labelle, Paul Anka, Perry Como, Ray Charles, Rosemary Clooney, Smokey Robinson, Willie Nelson . . .

Maybe you'll be next!

THE NIGHT BEFORE CHRISTMAS CAR-I-OKE

TRACK 9

If you've stopped caroling long enough to read the stories and facts in this book, you'll know that Christmas evolved over many centuries through many cultures. Yet much that defines the holiday we celebrate today appeared virtually overnight, in New York City in 1822, when Clement C. Moore wrote the poem he called "A Visit from Saint Nicholas." A scholar, author, and real-estate developer, Moore penned this "mere trifle" on Christmas Eve, during a sleigh ride from Greenwich Village to his country estate in Chelsea—or so legend has it*—as a gift to his six children. That might have been the end of it but for a family friend who surreptitiously sent it to an out-of-town newspaper, the *Sentinel.* They published the poem on December 23, 1823, and the rest is history.

In the poem, Moore not only created the Santa Claus we've come to know and love—before Moore, Saint Nick was a reedy, often disagreeable-looking fellow—but also the indelible image of a cozy family holiday centered around a magical being who delivers presents to children. Who since Moore hasn't grown up imagining hearing the pitter-patter of hoofbeats on the rooftop?

---

* LEGEND INDEED • Recent literary detective work offers a good theory as to why Clement Moore dismissed the significance of "A Visit from Saint Nicholas"—he might not be the author! Some scholars now believe the poem was written by Henry Livingston Jr., one of the first New Yorkers to enlist in the Revolutionary Army in 1775 and a distant ancestor of both Presidents Bush.

THE NIGHT BEFORE CHRISTMAS CAR-I-OKE

'Twas the night before Christmas, when all through the house
Not a creature was stirring, not even a mouse;
The stockings were hung by the chimney with care,
In hopes that St. Nicholas soon would be there;
The children were nestled all snug in their beds,
While visions of sugar-plums danced in their heads;
And mamma in her kerchief, and I in my cap,
Had just settled down for a long winter's nap.

Refrain:
Dasher, Dancer, Prancer, Vixen;
Comet, Cupid, Donner, Blitzen.

When out on the lawn there arose such a clatter,
I sprang from the bed to see what was the matter.
Away to the window I flew like a flash,
Tore open the shutters and threw up the sash.
The moon on the breast of the new-fallen snow
Gave the lustre of mid-day to objects below,
When, what to my wondering eyes should appear,
But a miniature sleigh, and eight tiny reindeer.

Repeat refrain

MUSH!

Reindeer, which thrive in the coldest places on the planet, have been domesticated by humans for thousands of years, and trained to pull sleighs of cargo and people. There continue to be native people—in Scandinavia, across northern Eurasia, in Alaska—who depend on the reindeer herds for their living.

RUB-A-DUB-DUB

Reggae and its uptempo predecessor, ska, are two musical styles that grew out of Jamaica. But Jamaica also contributed to the birth of an even more popular musical genre—rap. Remember the old 45s? (Parents may have to explain.) In Jamaica it was common for a full reggae single to be released on side A, and an instrumental version of the song—called a "dub"—on side B. A Jamaican MC named Daddy U-Roy started talking and chatting over the dub side. In the early 1970s, this style reached folks

With a little old driver, so lively and quick,
I knew in a moment it must be St. Nick.
More rapid than eagles his coursers they came,
And he whistled, and shouted, and called them by name;
"Now, Dasher! now, Dancer! now, Prancer and Vixen!
On, Comet! on, Cupid! on, Donner and Blitzen!
To the top of the porch! to the top of the wall!
Now dash away! dash away! dash away all!"

Repeat refrain

As dry leaves that before the wild hurricane fly,
When they meet with an obstacle, mount to the sky,
So up to the house-top the coursers they flew,
With the sleigh full of toys, and St. Nicholas too.
And then, in a twinkling, I heard on the roof
The prancing and pawing of each little hoof.
As I drew in my hand, and was turning around,
Down the chimney St. Nicholas came with a bound.

Repeat refrain

He was dressed all in fur, from his head to his foot,
And his clothes were all tarnished with ashes and soot;
A bundle of toys he had flung on his back,
And he looked like a peddler just opening his pack.
His eyes—how they twinkled! His dimples, how merry!

24

His cheeks were like roses, his nose like a cherry!
His droll little mouth was drawn up like a bow,
And the beard of his chin was as white as the snow.

Repeat refrain

The stump of a pipe he held tight in his teeth,
And the smoke it encircled his head like a wreath;
He had a broad face and a little round belly,
That shook when he laughed, like a bowlful of jelly.
He was chubby and plump, a right jolly old elf,
And I laughed when I saw him, in spite of myself;
A wink of his eye and a twist of his head,
Soon gave me to know I had nothing to dread.

Repeat refrain

He spoke not a word, but went straight to his work,
And filled all the stockings; then turned with a jerk,
And laying his finger aside of his nose,
And giving a nod, up the chimney he rose;
He sprang to his sleigh, to his team gave a whistle,
And away they all flew like the down of a thistle.
But I heard him exclaim, ere he drove out of sight,
"Happy Christmas to all, and to all a good-night."

Repeat refrain

of Caribbean descent in the Bronx, New York, and into the hands of DJ Cool Herc and other party DJs. When the 1979 song "Rapper's Delight" by the Sugarhill Gang reached #36 on the *Billboard* charts, this new music was announced to the world, and hip-hop culture was born.

SINGER'S NOTE

Here's a brand-new song for singing along. Kids, there are two parts requiring your best performance. On the chorus, pretend to be more and more upset, until you shout out "IT'S IMPOSSIBLE TO SLEEP!" And in the bridge, try to sing with a whisper in your voice to make it suspenseful. Pretend you really are sneaking down the steps and don't want to be caught!

BAH, HUMBUG!

TRACK 10

Remember that feeling? You were so excited, the thought of sleep seemed inconceivable, impossible! There you were, the night before Christmas, fully caught up in the thrill of Santa's impending visit, flipping back and forth on the pillow, dreaming of . . . stuff. And if you were a certain age, every creak in the floorboards, every muffled voice coming from downstairs, every moment of sudden wakefulness—you must have dozed off, but it's still night, but what time is it?—was magic to be investigated. Yet somehow you did fall asleep, and somehow when the first flush of morning light filtered in through the blinds, it took at least one delicious second to remember what morning it was. Then came the flood of excitement: It's *that* morning! And now I can get up!

Here's a song, based on a true experience, about some kids who didn't stay asleep. They tiptoed down in the middle of the night, plugged in the Christmas tree lights, and sat reverently before the seeming mountain of gifts. (Kids, don't try this at home!) The next thing they knew, their parents had appeared. But instead of being angry, they cozied up with their kids around the tree and started a new tradition: opening presents in the middle of the night.

BAH, HUMBUG!

Words and music by David Schiller

First verse:

Mama said, no sneaking, no peeking around
    the Christmas tree
Bah, humbug! Bah, humbug!
Papa said, got to get to bed early on Christmas Eve
Bah, humbug! Bah, humbug!

Chorus:

Why, why, why must we go to bed?
We don't care what papa said,
We can't sleep!
We won't sleep!
We'll never sleep!
IT'S IMPOSSIBLE TO SLEEP!!!

Second verse:

Mama said, settle down now, be good girls and boys,
Bah, humbug! Bah, humbug!
Papa said, I'm coming up if I hear one more noise,
Bah, humbug! Bah, humbug!

Repeat chorus

THE DICKENS

Quick! Can you name the famous character who uses the phrase "Bah! Humbug!"? Of course, it's Ebenezer Scrooge. The story of Scrooge learning the true meaning of Christmas is one of the most popular stories ever told. It also is almost directly responsible for shifting Christmas from a public holiday to a family holiday—and bestowing on all of us the feeling of charity toward the less fortunate that is so integral to what we now call the Christmas Spirit.

OFFBEAT

Reggae is a style of music that originated in Jamaica and is characterized by its strong, leading bass line and springy rhythm accented on the offbeat. Reggae grew out of a delicious musical stew with its beginnings in *mento* (Jamaican calypso) and American R&B (rhythm and blues), which evolved into ska, which evolved into a style called rock steady, which then—in the late 1960s and early 1970s, in the hands of artists like Bob Marley and the Wailers and Toots and the Maytals—became reggae.

Bridge:

It's just so hard to wait for Christmas
The night drags on and on and on.
Here we go, tiptoe down the stairs
Plug in the tree, it shines so bright
Quiet now, the whole house is snoring
We're all along in the middle of the night
See the presents, piled like a mountain!
Boxes and boxes, all green and red
Pick one up, shake it and smell it—
HEY! PUT THAT DOWN! GET BACK TO BED!!!

Third verse:

Mama said, come here, kids, gather 'round the Christmas tree
Merry Christmas, merry Christmas
Papa said, O why not, here's a present to you from me,
                    Merry Christmas, merry Christmas!

Last chorus:

Boy, oh, boy, oh, what a Christmas Eve
Spent the night 'round the Christmas
    tree
Now we got to sleep,
We really want to sleep,
Can we go to sleep?
WE NEED TO SLEEP!!!!

THE TWELVE DAYS OF CHRISTMAS

TRACK **11**

Many versions of "The Twelve Days of Christmas" exist. The song we now sing was first published in England in 1842. A Scottish version lists among the gifts an Arabian baboon, and a version from France is nearly all food: "One boneless stuffing, two breasts of veal, three joints of beef, four pig's trotters, five legs of mutton," and so on. In keeping with the song's inventive, whimsical spirit, we suggest a fill-in-the-blank game. If you get stuck, just pretend you're making your list for Santa—and you know he can bring you anything in the world!

For most verses, you just want to insert a noun and an adjective—"rocking skateboards." Even better, use words that begin with the same sounds, which is called alliteration: "sizzling skateboards." Then you could flip it, the way the original does—"skateboards a-sizzling." Don't be reluctant to change words around to get the best lines. And don't be afraid to be nonsensical. "The Twelve Days of Christmas" is a long song, but it's a lot of fun to sing because it becomes a long, rolling, poetic incantation. Now, in addition, we can enjoy silliness, too.

WHO WROTE IT?

The authorship of this English carol is lost in the mists of time. The best guess as to when the song originated is the sixteenth century, an era when counting songs were popular, and when Christmas celebrations stretched over many days. The twelve days start on Christmas and extend to Epiphany, which marks the occasion of the Wise Men bringing their gifts to the baby Jesus.

THE TWELVE DAYS OF CHRISTMAS

On the first day of Christmas,

My true love sent to me,

A _____ in a(n) _____,
       noun   *adjective*

_____.
    noun

On the second day of Christmas,

My true love sent to me,

Two _____ _____,
       adjective   *noun*

And a _____.
         day 1

On the third day of Christmas,

My true love sent to me,

Three _____ _____,
        adjective   *noun*

Two _____,
        day 2

And a _____.
        day 1

On the fourth day of Christmas,

My true love sent to me,

Four _____ _____,
      adjective   *noun*

Three _____,
        day 3

Two _____,
        day 2

And a _____,
        day 1

On the fifth day of Christmas,

My true love sent to me,

Five _____ _____,
      adjective   *noun*

Four _____,
        day 4

Three _____,
        day 3

Two _____,
        day 2

And a _____.
        day 1

On the sixth day of Christmas,

My true love sent to me,

Six _____ a-_____,
      noun   *verbing*

Five _____,
        day 5

Four _____,
        day 4

Three _____,
        day 3

Two _____,
        day 2

And a _____.
        day 1

On the seventh day of Christmas,

My true love sent to me,

Seven _____ a-_____,
      noun   *verbing*

Six _____,
        day 6

Five _____,
        day 5

Four _____ ,
    day 4
Three _____ ,
    day 3
Two _____ ,
    day 2
And a _____ .
    day 1

On the eighth day of Christmas,

My true love sent to me,

Eight _____ a-_____ ,
    noun   *verbing*
Seven _____ ,
    day 7
Six _____ ,
    day 6
Five _____ ,
    day 5
Four _____ ,
    day 4
Three _____ ,
    day 3
Two _____ ,
    day 2
And a _____ .
    day 1

On the ninth day of Christmas,

My true love sent to me,

Nine _____ _____ ,
    noun   *verbing*
Eight _____ ,
    day 8
Seven _____ ,
    day 7
Six _____ ,
    day 6

Five _____ ,
    day 5
Four _____ ,
    day 4
Three _____ ,
    day 3
Two _____ ,
    day 2
And a _____ .
    day 1

On the tenth day of Christmas,

My true love sent to me,

Ten _____ a-_____ ,
    noun   *verbing*
Nine _____ ,
    day 9
Eight _____ ,
    day 8
Seven _____ ,
    day 7
Six _____ ,
    day 6
Five _____ ,
    day 5
Four _____ ,
    day 4
Three _____ ,
    day 3
Two _____ ,
    day 2
And a _____ .
    day 1

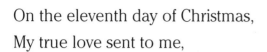

On the eleventh day of Christmas,

My true love sent to me,

Eleven _____ _____,
       noun   *verbing*

Ten _____,
           day 10

Nine _____,
           day 9

Eight _____,
           day 8

Seven _____,
           day 7

Six _____,
           day 6

Five _____,
           day 5

Four _____,
           day 4

Three _____,
           day 3

Two _____,
           day 2

And a _____.
           day 1

On the twelfth day of Christmas,

My true love sent to me,

Twelve _____ _____,
       noun   *verbing*

Eleven _____,
           day 11

Ten _____,
           day 10

Nine _____,
           day 9

Eight _____,
           day 8

Seven _____,
           day 7

Six _____,
           day 6

Five _____,
           day 5

Four _____,
           day 4

Three _____,
           day 3

Two _____,
           day 2

And a _____.
           day 1

THE TWELVE DAYS OF CHRISTMAS

My oh my, how times have changed. No Game Boys, no iPod Minis—not even a pet rock! Back in the old days, Christmas lists were a lot less . . . fun. Of course, we're kidding. It's doubtful that French hens and leaping lords were given to anyone for the holidays. But it is fun to sing. Here are the original "Twelve Days of Christmas." Hit the repeat button on the CD player, and sing it again.

Day 1: A partridge in a pear tree
Day 2: Two turtle doves
Day 3: Three French hens
Day 4: Four calling birds
Day 5: Five golden rings
Day 6: Six geese a-laying
Day 7: Seven swans a-swimming
Day 8: Eight maids a-milking
Day 9: Nine ladies dancing
Day 10: Ten lords a-leaping
Day 11: Eleven pipers piping
Day 12: Twelve drummers drumming

GATHER 'ROUND THE YULE TUBE, or THE TWELVE NIGHTS OF CHRISTMAS

Climb onto the couch, everyone. Turn down the lights, pass the popcorn. Settle in to the newest tradition to be embraced by millions of families: the Christmas movie. Santa Claus debuted on the silver screen back in 1898, starring in a two-minute English feature that used trick photography. Thomas Edison oversaw a film version of "The Night Before Christmas"—shot in 1914, it was the first movie to use a screenplay. But it was just after World War II that Hollywood kicked into full gear making movies just for the holidays—though it took them a while to figure it all out: *Miracle on 34th Street* was released in the long hot days of the summer of 1947.

So, are Christmas movies a part of your family holiday? Here's a little matching quiz to see how well you know the best-loved holiday stories.

1. In this classic fish-out-of-water comedy, a human baby falls into Santa's sack and is transported back to the North Pole, where he's raised as one of the elves.

2. Santa dies in a fall from a roof, so a Scrooge-like divorced dad takes his place. The next morning, Dad thinks it was all just a dream—until his out-of-control body starts putting on weight and growing a prodigious beard.

3. A widowed father struggles to keep food on the table and doesn't have much time for his daughter, Jessica. But when she finds an injured reindeer and imagines that it is part of Santa's sled crew, this plainspoken movie proves that a reindeer doesn't have to fly to be magical.

4. A pair of song-and-dance men hook up with a sister act to put on a big show and save the struggling resort owned by their beloved former army commander.

5. Is he or isn't he? A charming old man named Kris Kringle gets a job as a department store Santa, only to find his credentials under attack by everyone from a little girl to store management.

6. A perfect kid's-eye view of Christmas in the 1940s, centered around a desire so strong the boy can taste it—to wake up and find a Daisy brand Red Ryder BB rifle under the tree.

7. A dreamer is frustrated at every turn and thinks his life is a failure, until an angel comes down to show him a scary vision—what life would have been like for the people he loves had he never been born.

8. A miserly businessman who despises the holiday is visited by three ghosts on Christmas Eve, who show him the truth about his lonely life and inspire him with the real meaning of Christmas.

9. The solemn leader of this beloved gang of kids faces one obstacle after another in an effort to mount a school Christmas pageant.

10. A special hero and his misfit buddies conspire to save Christmas, meeting along the way a colorful prospector, a snow monster, a legion of abandoned toys, and a skinny Santa.

11. A cuddly-as-a-cactus villain sneaks into a village on Christmas Eve and steals everything in sight, only to discover that the residents don't care—Christmas isn't about the stuff, it's about the spirit.

12. It's a musical! A fantasy! A horror movie! A comedy! And the only Disney movie in which Santa is kidnapped and roughed up —in this case, by the scary/funny guy from Halloweentown, Jack Skellington.

A. WHITE CHRISTMAS
B. A CHARLIE BROWN CHRISTMAS
C. THE GRINCH WHO STOLE CHRISTMAS
D. A CHRISTMAS STORY
E. PRANCER
F. ELF
G. RUDOLPH THE RED-NOSED REINDEER
H. A CHRISTMAS CAROL
I. THE NIGHTMARE BEFORE CHRISTMAS
J. MIRACLE ON 34TH STREET
K. THE SANTA CLAUSE
L. IT'S A WONDERFUL LIFE

1F. 2K. 3E. 4A. 5J. 6D. 7L. 8H. 9B. 10G. 11C. 12I

WHAT DO THEY KNOW?

"For dancers there is rather little in it, for art absolutely nothing, and for the artistic fate of our ballet, one more step downward."—EARLY REVIEWER ON *THE NUTCRACKER*

THE NUTCRACKER

Welcome to the Backseat Ballet Company! Obviously we can't sing *The Nutcracker*—ballets have no words—so instead we thought we'd have fun performing it. Here are three pieces, and some balletic ideas and movements for dancing with your seatbelt on.

But first, a bit of explanation for those of you who haven't seen *The Nutcracker.* The ballet begins with a Christmas Eve party at the grand Stahlbaum house in the shadow of the most extraordinary Christmas tree. Among those who welcome the guests are Clara and Fritz, the Stahlbaum children. One of the guests is Herr Drosselmeyer, the children's godfather, who brings Clara a beautiful nutcracker. Fritz is somewhat jealous and breaks it. Clara is heartbroken. After all the guests leave, she sneaks back to the tree and falls asleep with the nutcracker in her arms.

At midnight, mysterious things begin to happen. Clara shrinks while the tree grows higher and higher. Toys come to life, and the room fills with an army of mice led by the fierce Mouse King. The Nutcracker and his toy soldiers are no match for the mice until Clara throws her slipper at the Mouse King and ends the battle.

Happily, Clara and the Nutcracker, now a prince, go off and visit enchanted lands—the Land of Snow and the Land of Sweets. After the beautiful dance of the Sugar Plum Fairy and the Cavalier, Clara awakens, the nutcracker in her arms.

Tap, tap, tap—do you hear the conductor's wand calling the orchestra to attention? Here we go!

MARCH

TRACK 12

Welcome to the Christmas party! The parade of guests is arriving, all dressed up and excited. Now you're making your entrance. You are an adult, and dignified, so your movement has to be formal and elegant. You don't want to fling your arms around wildly. (Not only is that not in character, but you might whack your brother or sister!) If you're alone in the backseat you can pretend that you're saying hello to the other guests. If you're sharing the backseat, you can perform a pas de deux (step for two). Think of a pas de deux as a movement conversation.

- Moving in time to the music, turn your head gracefully from side to side like you're saying hello to lots of people in a crowded room. Smile and use your eyes to express happiness. Your entire face has to come alive.
- Add your hands and arms. As you turn your head to the right, lift your right hand off your lap and open your palm. Keep your movement smooth.
- Do the same movements to your left.
- Now add your feet. As you turn your head and open your palm to your right, lift your right knee and touch your right toes lightly to the floor. Really stretch your foot. Now do the same movements to your left side. Go from side to side.

DANCER'S TIP #1

Though they at first look mysterious, all the movements that you see in a ballet performance come from movements that you do almost every day in real life. For example, a grand jeté is really just a big leap.

DANCER'S TIP #2

Listen to the music and see if you can pick out sounds and rhythms that suggest the events happening in the story. That way, when you do the movements here, you can imagine that you're really one of the characters.

DANCER'S TIP #3

A lot of the movement is a combination of ballet steps and mime. Mime is when dancers express emotions and events with exaggeration, like when you play a game of charades. In real life, for example, when you greet someone you haven't seen for a long time, you might give them a nice hug and a smile. But a dancer's hug and smile have to be big enough so that everyone everywhere in the audience can see what's happening.

Ready to try a variation? Pretend to be a little kid, with giggling and whispering:

- Mime a whisper to the person sitting next to you. Cup your hands next to your mouth so no one else can hear. Move from side to side in rhythm with the music. (If you're performing a pas de deux, the two of you should pay close attention to each other's movements so that your responses to each other make sense.)
- Mime laughter by moving your shoulders up and down, in rhythm with the music. Sway from side to side. Be sure to smile.
- Roll your hands around each other, like you're rolling up a ball of yarn.
- Tap your feet quickly, like you're running.

Ready to put all these movements together?
1. Whisper to your right.
2. Whisper to your left.
3. Mime laughter and sway to your right.
4. Mime laughter and sway to your left.
5. Roll your hands and tap your feet.
6. Repeat.

COFFEE

TRACK 13

When you hear the word *coffee,* you think of dark, steaming hot liquid. When you listen to the music composed for this dance, which has an exotic Arabian flavor, you might imagine coffee simmering in a pot. The movement captures this vision. It's silky and mysterious.

- Moving slowly and smoothly, like a snake slithering through grass, lift your right elbow toward the ceiling of the car. Let your lower arm and hand hang down at your side. As you're lifting your elbow, lean your torso and head to the left.
- When you've lifted your elbow a little higher than your shoulder, lower your arm to your side. As you lower your elbow, lean your torso and head to your right.
- Do the same movements using your left arm.
- Now go from one side to the other. One arm moves up as the other moves down.

Variation:

- Try performing the same arm movements with your arms in front of your torso. Which ways can you move your torso and head?

DANCER'S TIP #4

Before you begin, place your hands in your lap and sit up straight in your seat. A dancer must never slouch! And take off your shoes so you can point your feet.

DANCER'S TIP #5

When you listen to the music, you may have your own ideas about movements you'd like to do. You may enjoy improvising, which means making up movements on the spur of the moment. So go ahead, let the music move you!

TREPAK

This is a Russian folk dance. The movement is very athletic and the rhythms are bold.

- Put your feet flat on the floor in front of you.
- Bend both of your elbows and place one arm on top of the other. Keep your fingers stretched and straight.
- Hold this position and lift your arms forward until they're as high as your chest. Keep your back very straight and hold your head high, like a proud stallion.
- Lift your right foot and tap your right heel against the floor.
- Lift your left foot and tap your left heel against the floor.
- Now go from side to side: right heel, left heel, moving in time to the music.

Variation:

- Right heel, left heel
- Both heels at the same time
- Repeat

Pas de Deux:

Perform the movements in unison with your partner, then try doing them in opposition: When you tap your right heel, your partner taps his or her left.

NOW, TAKE A BOW!

An Unexpected Holiday Tradition

Today we know *The Nutcracker* as an enchanting ballet that is performed every year at Christmastime to the wide-eyed delight of audiences around the world. But it took many years for the tradition to take hold.

The story told in *The Nutcracker* has its origins in a dark tale from the early nineteenth century called "The Nutcracker and the Mouse King," by the German writer E.T.A. Hoffman. It was written as a kind of bitter fairy tale for adults who have lost sight of their dreams—Hoffman even cautioned readers that it might frighten children. Later, the famed French writer Alexander Dumas adapted the tale as a children's story, which was turned into a full-length ballet by the Russian Imperial Ballet in 1892, with a score by Peter Ilyich Tchaikovsky. Curiously, while reviewers panned the piece, average theatergoers came back night after night. Something took root.

Eventually the ballet left Russia and fell into the hands of one of the most famous choreographers of all time, George Balanchine, who found its magical soul— its Sugar Plum fairies and miraculously growing Christmas tree—and turned it into the ballet we know and love today. It had its premier on February 2, 1954, and is the most lasting dance hit in history, as every year some two hundred companies around the United States perform *The Nutcracker* at Christmastime.

O CHRISTMAS TREE

Greenness is not the best indicator of freshness. Growers routinely spray Christmas trees with color. But here's one test for a fresh tree: Raise it a few inches and let it drop on its butt end. Needles should not fall off. Another freshness test is to lightly pull a branch through your fingers—most needles should stay on.

Does your family have a favorite tree? Here are some of ours. **Fraser Fir:** Treasured for its soft, silver-green needles and classic Christmas-tree shape, with sturdy

THE "O" MEDLEY

Attention, carolers! Here is a medley of traditional carols that begin with the word "O." We've chosen four of the best known: the tender "O Little Town of Bethlehem," the reverential "O Holy Night," the joyous "O Come, All Ye Faithful," and ending with the rousing "O Christmas Tree." Our CD includes four bonus tracks, which are the complete recordings of each song. Full lyrics are on pages 44 to 47; the bonus tracks are numbers 19 to 22, at the end of the disc.

THE "O" MEDLEY

O little town of Bethlehem,
How still we see thee lie!
Above thy deep and dreamless sleep
The silent stars go by.
Yet in thy dark streets shineth
The everlasting Light;
The hopes and fears of all the years
Are met in thee tonight.

O Holy night, the stars are brightly shining;
It is the night of the dear Savior's birth.
Long lay the world in sin and error pining,
Till He appeared and the soul felt His worth.
A thrill of hope, the weary world rejoices

For yonder breaks a new and glorious morn.
Fall on your knees! Oh, hear the angel voices!
O night divine! O night when Christ was born!
O night divine! O night when Christ was born.

O come, all ye faithful, joyful and
	triumphant,
O come ye, O come ye, to Bethlehem.
Come and behold Him, born the King
	of angels;
O come, let us adore Him,
O come, let us adore Him,
O come, let us adore Him,
	Christ the Lord.

O Christmas tree! O Christmas tree!
Thy leaves are so unchanging;
O Christmas tree! O Christmas tree!
Thy leaves are so unchanging;
Not only green when summer's
	here,
But also when 'tis cold and
	drear.
O Christmas tree!
	O Christmas tree!
Thy leaves are so unchanging!

branches. **Colorado Blue Spruce:** Nice shape, strong limbs, and lovely bluish color. **Scotch Pine:** A tightly branched tree known for its excellent needle retention, even if it dries up. **Balsam Fir:** Ah, the fragrance of evergreen woods, and a beautiful dark green color, too. **Norway Spruce:** Beautiful, but must be cut fresh and properly watered. **Grand Fir:** Have room for a 300 footer? **Eastern White Pine:** Often the evergreen of choice for use in garlands, wreaths, and centerpieces.

Here are the individual songs of the "O" Medley in their wonderful entirety.

O LITTLE TOWN
OF BETHLEHEM

TRACK 19

First verse:

O little town of Bethlehem,
How still we see thee lie!
Above thy deep and dreamless sleep,
The silent stars go by.
Yet in thy dark streets shineth
The everlasting Light;
The hopes and fears of all the years
Are met in thee tonight.

Second verse:

For Christ is born of Mary,
And gathered all above,
While mortals sleep, the angels keep
Their watch of wondering love.
O morning stars, together
Proclaim the holy birth,
And praises sing to God the King,
And peace to men on earth!

Third verse:

How silently, how silently,
The wondrous Gift is giv'n;
So God imparts to human hearts
The blessings of His Heav'n.
No ear may hear His coming,
But in this world of sin,
Where meek souls will receive Him still,
The dear Christ enters in.

Fourth verse:

Where children pure and happy
Pray to the blessèd Child,
Where misery cries out to Thee,

44

Son of the mother mild;
Where charity stands watching
And faith holds wide the door,
The dark night wakes, the glory breaks,
And Christmas comes once more.

O HOLY NIGHT

TRACK 20

First verse:

O Holy night, the stars are brightly shining
It is the night of the dear Savior's birth.
Long lay the world in sin and error pining
Till He appeared and
    the soul felt His worth.
A thrill of hope, the weary world rejoices
For yonder breaks a new and
    glorious morn.

Refrain:

Fall on your knees!
    Oh, hear the angel voices!
O night divine!
    O night when Christ was born!
O night divine! O night, O night divine!

Second verse:

Led by the light of faith serenely beaming
With glowing hearts
    by His cradle we stand.
So led by light of a star sweetly gleaming
Here came the wise men
    from the Orient land.
The King of Kings lay in lowly manger
In all our trials born to be our friend.

Repeat refrain

Third verse:

Truly He taught us to love one another
His law is love and His gospel is peace.
Chains shall He break,
    for the slave is our brother
And in His name
    all oppression shall cease.
Sweet hymns of joy in grateful
    chorus rise we
Let all within us praise His holy name.

Repeat refrain

O COME, ALL YE FAITHFUL   TRACK **21**

First verse:

O come, all ye faithful,
     joyful and triumphant,
O come ye, O come ye to Bethlehem.
Come and behold Him,
     born the King of angels.

Refrain:

O come, let us adore Him,
O come, let us adore Him,
O come, let us adore Him, Christ the Lord.

Second verse:

Sing, choirs of angels, sing in exultation;
O sing, all ye citizens of heaven above!
Glory to God, all glory in the highest.

Repeat refrain

Third verse:

See how the shepherds,
     summoned to His cradle,
Leaving their flocks, draw nigh to gaze;
We too will thither bend
     our joyful footsteps.

Repeat refrain

O CHRISTMAS TREE

TRACK 22

First verse:

O Christmas tree! O Christmas tree!
Thy leaves are so unchanging.
O Christmas tree! O Christmas tree!
Thy leaves are so unchanging.
Not only green when summer's here,
But also when 'tis cold and drear.
O Christmas tree! O Christmas tree!
Thy leaves are so unchanging.

Second verse:

O Christmas tree! O Christmas tree!
Much pleasure thou can'st give me.
O Christmas tree! O Christmas tree!
Much pleasure thou can'st give me.
How often has the Christmas tree
Afforded me the greatest glee.
O Christmas tree! O Christmas tree!
Much pleasure thou can'st give me.

Third verse:

O Christmas tree! O Christmas tree!
Thy candles shine so brightly.
O Christmas tree! O Christmas tree!
Thy candles shine so brightly.
From base to summit, gay and bright,
There's only splendor for the sight.
O Christmas tree! O Christmas tree!
Thy candles shine so brightly.

Try a verse in the original German:

O Tannenbaum, O Tannenbaum,
Wie treu sind deine Blätter!
O Tannenbaum, O Tannenbaum,
Wie treu sind deine Blätter!
Du grünst nicht nur zur Sommerzeit,
Nein auch im Winter, wenn es schneit.
O Tannenbaum, O Tannenbaum,
Wie treu sind deine Blätter!

SILENT NIGHT

TRACK 16

SINGER'S NOTE

How low can you go? "Silent Night" is simple, beloved, and written in the most familiar of keys, C major, but it does present challenges. There's the slowly swooping "heavenly pe-e-e-EEEACE," and then the steep drop immediately following, landing more than a full octave lower.

One of the most beautiful songs ever written, "Silent Night" has a touching story to match. During a snowy day in Obendorf, Austria, in 1816, Father Joseph Mohr was called to bless the baby of one of his poorest parishioners. Deeply moved by the scene, he wrote a poem, "Stille Nacht" (German for "silent night"). Two years later, on Christmas Eve, Mohr gave the poem to his friend Franz Gruber, the village schoolmaster and organist. Gruber had spent a long, frustrating day trying to repair the church organ. Mohr handed him a guitar and the verses—and that very night the two of them sang "Stille Nacht" to the worshipful crowd in the Church of St. Nicholas (yes, named after *the* St. Nicholas). For years afterward, the song traveled anonymously throughout the region of Tyrol, then Austria and Germany, and finally to the United States. It took the curiosity of the King of Prussia to unearth the song's true author (though not its composer—that would take another century).

SILENT NIGHT

First verse:

Silent night, holy night!
  All is calm, all is bright.
  'Round yon virgin Mother and Child,
  Holy infant so tender and mild.

Sleep in heavenly peace,
Sleep in heavenly peace.

Second verse:
Silent night, holy night!
Shepherds quake at the sight.
Glories stream from heaven afar.
Heav'nly hosts sing Alleluia;
Christ the Savior is born;
Christ the Savior is born.

Third verse:
Silent night, holy night!
Wondrous star, lend thy light!
With the angels, let us sing
Alleluia to our King!
Christ the Savior is here,
Jesus the Savior is here.

Fourth verse:
Silent night, holy night!
Son of God, love's pure light.
Radiant beams from Thy holy face,
With the dawn of redeeming grace.
Jesus, Lord, at Thy birth,
Jesus, Lord, at Thy birth.

ROLL OVER, BEETHOVEN

Even though Franz Gruber said he was the song's composer, almost everyone assumed that such a memorable work had to be the effort of a Beethoven, Mozart, or Haydn. Matters were finally cleared up in 1994, when a long-lost manuscript of the song was found in Joseph Mohr's handwriting, with the words "Melodie von Fr. Xav. Gruber" in the upper-right-hand corner.

FYI:

ORATORIO is a musical composition for voices and orchestra, that tells a sacred story without costumes, scenery, or dramatic action.

OPERA is a theatrical presentation in which a dramatic stage performance is set to music.

THE HALLELUJAH CHORUS

TRACK 🔟

If it's Christmas, it must be time for the *Messiah*. Greatly anticipated and treated almost as an antidote to the much decried commercialism of Christmas is the annual performance of Handel's masterpiece. One of the most popular musical works ever—it's been living near the top of the "charts" for the past 250 years!—Handel's *Messiah* is a three-act oratorio packed with hummable tunes, soaring arias, rousing choruses, and an overall feeling of touching the eternal.

George Frideric Handel was a German-born composer who found fame and fortune composing and performing operas in London, but by 1741 the fifty-six-year-old had fallen on hard times. Then two letters, and a burst of inspiration, changed all that. The first letter came from the Duke of Devonshire, inviting Handel to Dublin to produce a series of charity concerts. The second letter arrived from a wealthy Englishman named Charles Jennens, an eccentric who had written lyrics for some of Handel's operas and oratorios in the past. This time Jennens sent Handel a libretto compiled of passages from the Bible. Within three weeks, locked in his studio and claiming that he literally saw Heaven open up as he worked, Handel created the *Messiah*, and within a year performed it for the first time in Dublin. It was an instant success.

Over the years the *Messiah* has been performed, changed, and adapted (no less a composer than Mozart revised and re-orchestrated it to suit the Viennese). But it has always thrived. By the 1820s it had become *the* musical experience. Later in the century it was performed in the Crystal Palace Handel Festivals, where it ballooned with up to 3,000 singers performing for audiences in the tens of thousands!

HALLELUJAH

Hallelujah hallelujah hallelujah hallelujah hallelujah!
Hallelujah hallelujah hallelujah hallelujah hallelujah!
For the Lord God omnipotent reigneth,
Hallelujah hallelujah hallelujah hallelujah!
For the Lord God omnipotent reigneth,
Hallelujah hallelujah hallelujah hallelujah!
For the Lord God omnipotent reigneth,
Hallelujah hallelujah hallelujah hallelujah!
Hallelujah hallelujah hallelujah hallelujah!
Hallelujah hallelujah hallelujah hallelujah!
(For the Lord God omnipotent reigneth)
Hallelujah hallelujah hallelujah hallelujah!
For the Lord God omnipotent reigneth!
(Hallelujah hallelujah hallelujah hallelujah)
Hallelujah!
The kingdom of this world
Is become the kingdom of our Lord,
And of His Christ, and of His Christ,

> ## SINGER'S NOTE
>
> The *Messiah* in its entirety is three acts, and easily runs two-and-a-half hours long. For many people, though, the high point is the "Hallelujah" chorus at the end of Act II. Our Car-i-oke version is a sing-along, just like at a real performance. But you have to be ready to sing. *Really* sing. Have a good cough to clear the pipes, and let it rip!

PLEASE STAY SEATED!

If you've ever been to a performance of the *Messiah,* chances are good that the audience stood up during the "Hallelujah" chorus. This tradition started during one of the first performances of the piece. In the audience was King George II. When "Hallelujah" sounded, he leaped to his feet. (One rumor has it that he'd fallen asleep and was startled awake by the music.) Everyone else had to follow suit—no one can remain seated when a king stands!

And He shall reign forever and ever,
And He shall reign forever and ever,
And He shall reign forever and ever,
And He shall reign forever and ever.
King of kings, forever and ever, hallelujah, hallelujah!
And Lord of lords, forever and ever, hallelujah hallelujah!
King of kings, forever and ever, hallelujah, hallelujah!
And Lord of lords, forever and ever, hallelujah hallelujah!
King of kings, forever and ever, hallelujah, hallelujah!
And Lord of lords—
King of kings and Lord of lords—
And He shall reign,
And He shall reign,
And He shall reign,
He shall reign,
And He shall reign forever and ever!
King of kings forever and ever—
And Lord of lords hallelujah hallelujah!
And He shall reign forever and ever—
King of kings and Lord of lords,
King of kings and Lord of lords,
And He shall reign forever and ever—
Forever and ever and ever and ever,
(King of kings and Lord of lords)
Hallelujah hallelujah hallelujah hallelujah!
Hallelujah!

AULD LANG SYNE

TRACK 18

Here's your chance to show off for the grown-ups. "Auld Lang Syne," the "song that nobody knows," is tailor-made for Car-i-oke. After all, everyone can hum the melody, but who knows more than a fraction of the words? Taken from old Scottish ballads dating as far back as 1568, "Auld Lang Syne" was transcribed, polished, and published by the great Scottish poet Robert Burns in the mid 1790s. Loosely translated, "auld lang syne" means "times gone by," and singing this misty-eyed toast to old friends became part of the Scottish New Year tradition called Hogmanay.

AULD LANG SYNE

First verse:

Should auld acquaintance be forgot,
And never brought to mind?
Should auld acquaintance be forgot,
And days o' lang syne!

Chorus:

For auld lang syne, my dear
For auld lang syne,
We'll tak a cup o' kindness yet,
For auld lang syne!

GREAT BALLS OF FIRE!

We call it New Year's, but in Scotland it's called Hogmanay.

Among the most unusual customs of Hogmanay is a spectacular ceremony from Stonehaven, on the northeast coast: Huge fireballs, up to three feet in diameter and weighing twenty pounds, are attached to metal poles and carried and swung while people march through the streets. At the end of the ceremony, the fireballs that are still burning are swung out into the harbor.

THE NATIONAL ANTHEM OF NEW YEAR'S

You can answer the question of why "Auld Lang Syne" with just one name: Guy Lombardo. In 1929, while leading his orchestra at a New Year's Eve party in New York, he struck up "Auld Lang Syne" just before the midnight countdown. For nearly the next fifty years, Guy Lombardo and His Orchestra broadcast a New Year's Eve special from the Waldorf Astoria Hotel in New York City, and "Auld Lang Syne" became an institution.

Second verse:
We twa hae run about the braes,
And pu'd the gowans fine,
But we've wander'd mony a weary foot
Sin' auld lang syne.

Third verse:
We twa hae paidl't in the burn
Frae morning sun till dine,
But seas between us braid hae roar'd
Sin' auld lang syne.

Fourth verse:
And there's a hand, my trusty fiere,
And gie's a hand o' thine,
And we'll tak a right guid
    willie-waught
For auld lang syne!

Fifth verse:
And surely ye'll be your
    pint' stoup,
And surely I'll be mine!
And we'll tak a cup o'
    kindness yet
For auld lang syne!

AULD LANG SYNE (IN ENGLISH)

Can't tell your *stoup* from your *willie-waught?* Here's a translation of the Scottish.

TIMES LONG GONE

First verse:

Should old acquaintances be forgotten,
And never brought to mind?
Should old acquaintances
    be forgotten,
And days of long ago!

Chorus:

For old long ago, my dear
For old long ago,
We will take a cup of
    kindness yet
For old long ago.

Second verse:

We two have run about the hillsides
And pulled the daisies fine,
But we have wandered many a weary foot
For old long ago.

Third verse:

We two have paddled [waded] in the
    stream
From noon until dinner time,
But seas between us broad have roared
      Since old long ago.

Fourth verse:

And there is a hand, my
    trusty friend,
And give us a hand of yours,
And we will take a goodwill
    draught [of ale]
    For old long ago!

Fifth verse:

And surely you will pay for
    your pint,
And surely I will pay for mine!
And we will take a cup of kindness yet
For old long ago!

SINGING PRAISES

The brevity of this notice is in inverse proportion to how important the following people were in making this project happen: David Allender, Susan Bolotin, Paul Gamarello, Wayne Kirn, Mari Kraske, Katie Workman, Marta Jaremko, Larry Maltz, Rob and Julie Harari and their kids, the Sietz family, Tim Robinson, Lise Friedman, Paul Hanson, Asa, and, of course, Peter Workman. Many, many, many thanks.

RECORDING CREDITS

Produced by: Rob Harari
Executive Producer: David Schiller
Recorded at: HarariVille in Weehawken, NJ
Assistant: Steve Puig
Recording Administration: Julie Harari
Mastered by: Steve Vavagiakis at Bang Zoom
Arrangements composed and performed by: Rob Harari
Additional arrangements composed and performed by: Rick Cutler (songs 5, 6, 7, 11)
Midi programming for *The Nutcracker:* Christopher Speich
Drum loops/programming for "The Night Before Christmas Car-i-oke": Matt Sietz
Piano, percussion, keyboards, vocals (Hallelujah Chorus): Rob Harari
Guitars: Lawrence S. Maltz (songs 6, 7, 8, 9, 10, 11 and 16)
Bass: Bart Erbach (songs 8, 10)

Vocals

Angela Clemmons, Vaneese Y. Thomas, Darryl Tookes
Lead Vocal "Bah, Humbug!": Delia A. Kemph
Lead Vocal "The Night Before Christmas Car-i-oke": Darryl Tookes
Chorus on "Bah, Humbug!" and "The Night Before Christmas Car-i-oke": Joe and Genna Harari, Theo and Clara Schiller, Mandi, Sarah Nicole and Shawn Sietz, Sage Schwer